BART SIMPSON™
SON OF HOMER

HARPER

NEW YORK • LONDON • TORONTO • SYDNEY

32000123688881

BART SIMPSON: SON OF HOMER

Collects Bart Simpson Comics 29, 30, 31, 32, 33

Copyright © 2006 and 2009 by
Bongo Entertainment, Inc. All rights reserved.
No part of this book may be used or reproduced in any manner whatsoever
without written permission except in the case of brief quotations
embodied in critical articles and reviews. For information address
HarperCollins Publishers,
10 East 53rd Street, New York, NY 10022.

FIRST EDITION
ISBN 978-0-06-169879-8

09 10 11 12 13 QWM 10 9 8 7 6 5 4 3 2

Publisher: Matt Groening
Creative Director: Bill Morrison
Managing Editor: Terry Delegeane
Director of Operations: Robert Zaugh
Art Director: Nathan Kane
Art Director Special Projects: Serban Cristescu
Production Manager: Christopher Ungar
Assistant Art Director: Chia-Hsien Jason Ho
Production/Design: Karen Bates, Nathan Hamill, Art Villanueva
Staff Artist: Mike Rote
Administration: Sherri Smith, Pete Benson
Legal Guardian: Susan A. Grode

Trade Paperback Concepts and Design: Serban Cristescu

Cover: Ryan Rivette, Dan Davis and Serban Cristescu

HarperCollins Editors: Hope Innelli, Jeremy Cesarec

Contributing Artists:
Karen Bates, Jeff Brennan, John Costanza, Serban Cristescu, Mike DeCarlo, John Delaney,
Nathan Hamill, Jason Ho, James Lloyd, Nathan Kane, Bill Morrison, Joey Nilges, Phyllis Novin,
Phil Ortiz, Andrew Pepoy, Ryan Rivette, Mike Rote, Howard Shum, Chris Ungar, Art Villanueva

Contributing Writers:
James W. Bates, Tony DiGerolamo, Evan Dorkin, Amanda McCann,
Jesse Leon McCann, Tom Peyer, Eric Rogers, Mary Trainor

PRINTED IN CANADA

CONTENTS

TONY DIGEROLAMO
SCRIPT

JASON HO
PENCILS & INKS

NATHAN HAMILL
COLORS

KAREN BATES
LETTERS

MATT GROENING PRESENTS

BART SIMPSON

in

BART COPS OUT

EARLY ONE MORNING...

JUST ONE STOP BEFORE WE GET TO WORK.

BUT WE ATE PANCAKES, EGGS, SAUSAGE, AND TWO TYPES OF BACON FOR BREAKFAST!

IT'S "TAKE YOUR SON TO WORK DAY," AND IT'S TIME FOR *WORK BREAKFAST!*

SHOULDN'T WE GET TO *WORK* BEFORE WE HAVE WORK BREAKFAST?

YOU HAVE SO MUCH TO LEARN.

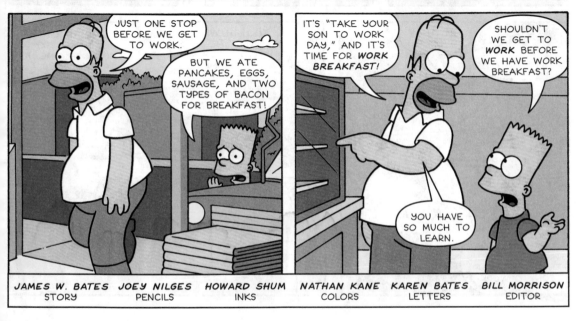

JAMES W. BATES
STORY

JOEY NILGES
PENCILS

HOWARD SHUM
INKS

NATHAN KANE
COLORS

KAREN BATES
LETTERS

BILL MORRISON
EDITOR

CHIEF WIGGUM & RALPH IN:
IF YOU CAN'T WIGGUM, JOIN 'EM!

TOM PEYER
SCRIPT

JAMES LLOYD
PENCILS

ANDREW PEPOY
INKS

NATHAN HAMILL
COLORS

KAREN BATES
LETTERS

BILL MORRISON
EDITOR

BART SIMPSON in K-BART

SUPERINTENDENT CHALMERS, HAVE I EVER TOLD YOU WHAT A COMPLETE AND UTTER *MORON* I THINK YOU ARE?

WHY NO, PRINCIPAL SKINNER, BUT WHY DON'T YOU TELL ME NOW, YOU *SPINELESS MOMMY'S BOY*?

ERIC ROGERS SCRIPT   **MIKE DECARLO** PENCILS   **PHYLLIS NOVIN** INKS   **NATHAN HAMILL** COLORS   **KAREN BATES** LETTERS   **BILL MORRISON** EDITOR

THERE ARE SEVERAL WORDS I COULD USE TO DESCRIBE WHAT A *LOSER* YOU ARE, CHALMERS, BUT THERE ARE CHILDREN LISTENING!

SEYMOUR, YOU'RE RIGHT... I *AM* A LOSER! I NEED TO BE *PUNISHED*!

WELL, I HAVE JUST THE TONIC FOR YOUR SICKNESS...MY TRUSTY PADDLE! NOW DROP YOUR CHINOS AND *BEND OVER*!

YES, SIR!

DID I MENTION I'LL *ALSO* GIVE YOU EACH A DVD COPY OF *THE COMPLETE FIRST SEASON OF "THE ITCHY AND SCRATCHY SHOW"?*

SIMPSON, GET A HOLD OF YOURSELF, DUDE!

MMMM... COMPLETE FIRST SEASON...

SIGN THE CONTRACT, OR YOU'LL BE SORRY!

NO WAY! WE'RE NOT SELLING OUT TO ANYONE!

SUIT YOURSELF, YOU LITTLE MUSH-BRAINED SQUAWK BOXES. WE'LL SEE WHO'S STANDING WHEN THIS IS ALL OVER.

BIRCH BARLOW CAN'T KEEP US FROM DOING OUR SHOW...CAN HE?

I DON'T KNOW. THAT GUY'S GOT SOME SERIOUSLY POWERFUL FRIENDS.

THE REPUBLICAN PARTY?

THE MOB?

TOUGHER. *RUSSELL CROWE!*

I'M SURE WE HAVE NOTHING TO WORRY ABOUT.

YEAH. HE'S JUST TRYING TO SCARE US IS ALL.

27

NELSON, HOW ARE WE GOING TO WIN AGAINST BARLOW? HE'S ONE OF THE MOST POWERFUL PEOPLE IN TOWN!

HE WASN'T ALWAYS A BIG SHOT, AND I HAVE *PROOF!*

"WHEN WE WERE GETTING THE SHOW READY TO AIR, I DECIDED TO FIND OUT HOW A RADIO STATION OPERATES. SO I INTERNED AT KDRK, THE STUDENT-RUN STATION AT SPRINGFIELD UNIVERSITY."

...THAT WAS "MIRROR IN THE BATHROOM" BY THE ENGLISH BEAT, CLOSING OUT ANOTHER RAD SET ON *THE NEW WAVE WONDER HOUR!* WE'LL BE RIGHT BACK AFTER WE PAY SOME BILLS...

WHAT DO *THESE* DO?

DON'T *TOUCH* ANYTHING! IF YOU WANT TO DO SOME-THING, WHY DON'T YOU GO IN THE BACK AND ORGANIZE THE TAPES OF OLD SHOWS?

"SO THAT'S WHAT I DID."

"THE HAPPENIN' WITH BIRCH-TREE BARLOW AND THE BEAUTIFUL BOHEMIANS"?!

"I TOOK THE TAPES HOME AND LISTENED TO THEM. IT TURNS OUT THEY WERE OF *BARLOW* DOING A SHOW WHEN HE WAS IN COLLEGE!"

THIS IS BIRCH-TREE BARLOW WITH MY BEAUTIFUL BOHEMIANS, AND WE'RE HERE TO LET EVERYONE KNOW IT'S COOL TO TAKE OFF YOUR CLOTHES, HUG A TREE, AND TELL *THE MAN* WHAT HE CAN DO WITH HIS MATERIAL POSSESSIONS!

GROOVY, BIRCH!

FAR OUT, BIRCH BABY!

HE WAS IN FAVOR OF EVERY-THING HE *HATES* TODAY!

WHICH MEANS WE'VE GOT SOME AMMUNITION, DUDE!

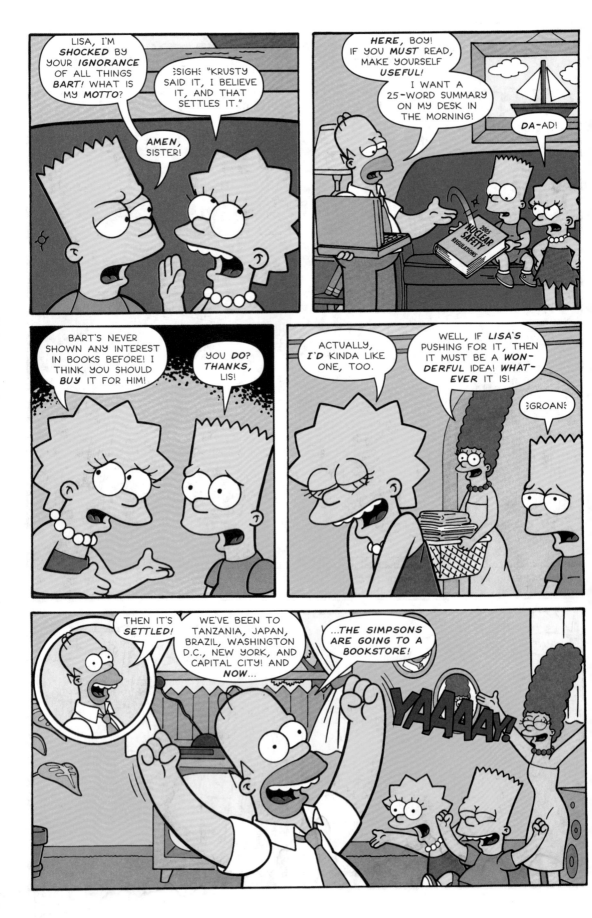

33

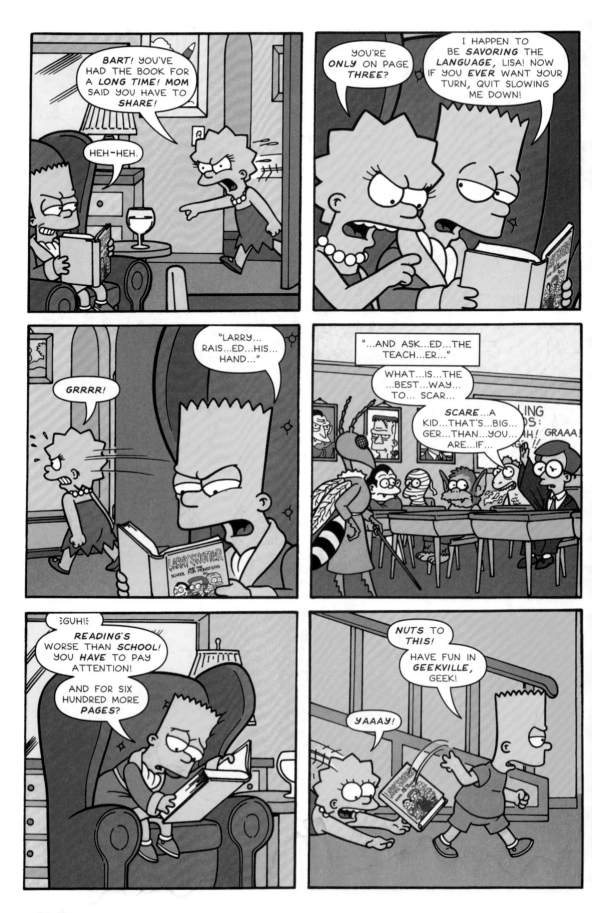

36

THE SECRET LIFE OF BART SIMPSON

MCBART! YOU'RE A *COP*, NOT A *TEST PILOT*!

IT'S *CERTAIN DEATH* TO FLY THIS EXPERIMENTAL NANO-PLANE!

STEP ASIDE, JIMBO!

LORD DEATHBOTTOM WILL TRIGGER DER *GIRL-GERM BOMB* IN 90 *SECONDS*! DIS PLANE'S MY *ONE CHANCE* TO *STOP* IT IN *TIME*!

MCBART, I'M NOT *ASKING*, I'M *ORDERING* YOU--

EAT MY SHORTS!

POW!

TOM PEYER
SCRIPT

JAMES LLOYD
PENCILS

ANDREW PEPOY
INKS

ART VILLANUEVA
COLORS

KAREN BATES
LETTERS

BILL MORRISON
EDITOR

45

TONY DIGEROLAMO
SCRIPT

RYAN RIVETTE
PENCILS

MIKE ROTE
INKS

ART VILLANUEVA
COLORS

KAREN BATES
LETTERS

BILL MORRISON
EDITOR

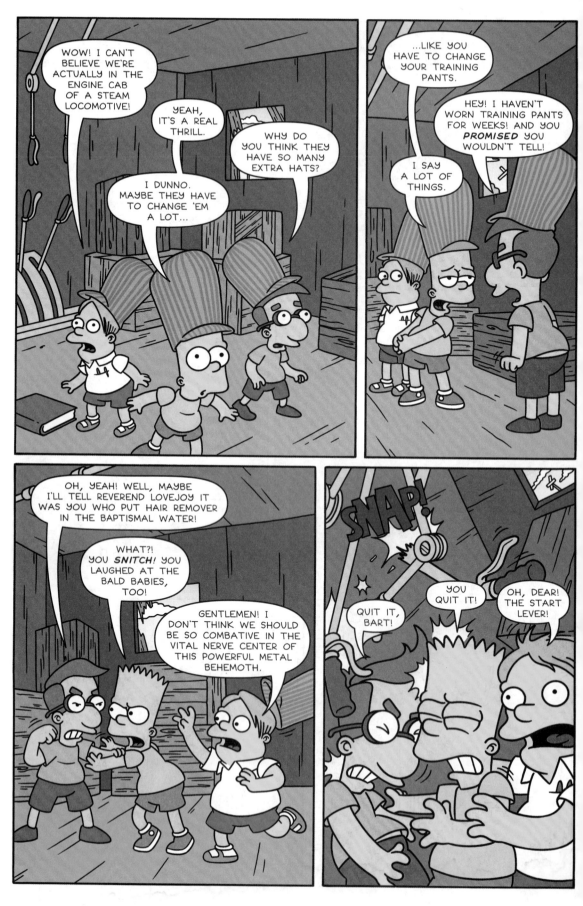

51

TONY DIGEROLAMO
SCRIPT

JASON HO
PENCILS & INKS

NATHAN HAMILL
COLORS

KAREN BATES
LETTERS

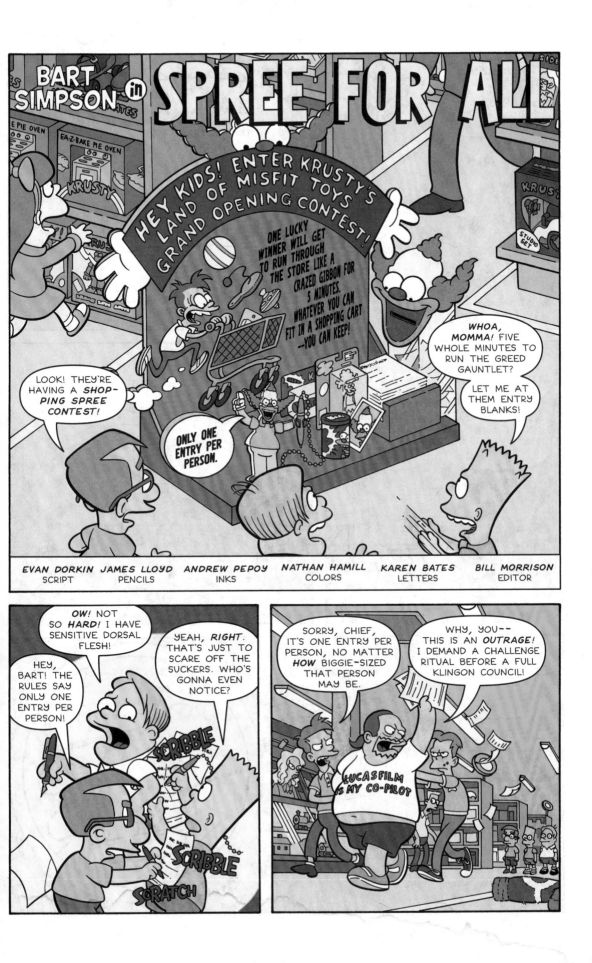

ON SECOND THOUGHT, I'LL JUST PUT IN *ONE* ENTRY. YOU KNOW, SPIRIT OF FAIR PLAY AND ALL THAT CRUD.

IF *I* WIN, THE FIRST THING I'LL GET IS THE RADIOACTIVE MAN VIDEO GAME THE SENATE IS TRYING TO BAN BECAUSE OF ADULT CONTENT.

THE FIRST THING *I'LL* DO IS *REGURGITATE* FROM SHEER EXCITEMENT! THEN I'D GRAB A STUFFED ANIMAL SIBLING SUBSTITUTE TO HUG DURING MY LONELIER MOMENTS.

DARE TO DREAM, DUDES. MAYBE I'LL GRAB THAT JUNK FOR YOU ON MY WAY TO AISLE 12, HOME OF THE NEW *KID-TASTIC KRUSTY-BOT* WITH 102 DIFFERENT FUNNY FUNCTIONS AND 12 HIDDEN DANGERS!

YEAH, RIGHT. HOW CAN YOU BE SO SURE YOU'LL WIN?

BECAUSE I'M BART SIMPSON, MAN. DON'T YOU *GET* IT?

...BREAKING REPORT OF WAR WITH NORTH KOREA, BUT FIRST...WE GO *LIVE* TO KRUSTY'S LAND OF MISFIT TOYS, WHERE THEY'RE ABOUT TO ANNOUNCE THE WINNER OF THE SHOPPING SPREE CONTEST!

HERE WE GO!

GOOD LUCK, KIDS!

HO-HO-*KAY*, FOLKS! IT'S THE MOMENT WE'VE *ALL* BEEN WAITING FOR, WHEN WE FIND OUT WHO GETS FIVE MINUTES TO RUN THROUGH KRUSTY'S LITTLE TAX DODGE!

HEH HEH. I MEAN, TOY STORE.

AND THE WINNER *IS*...

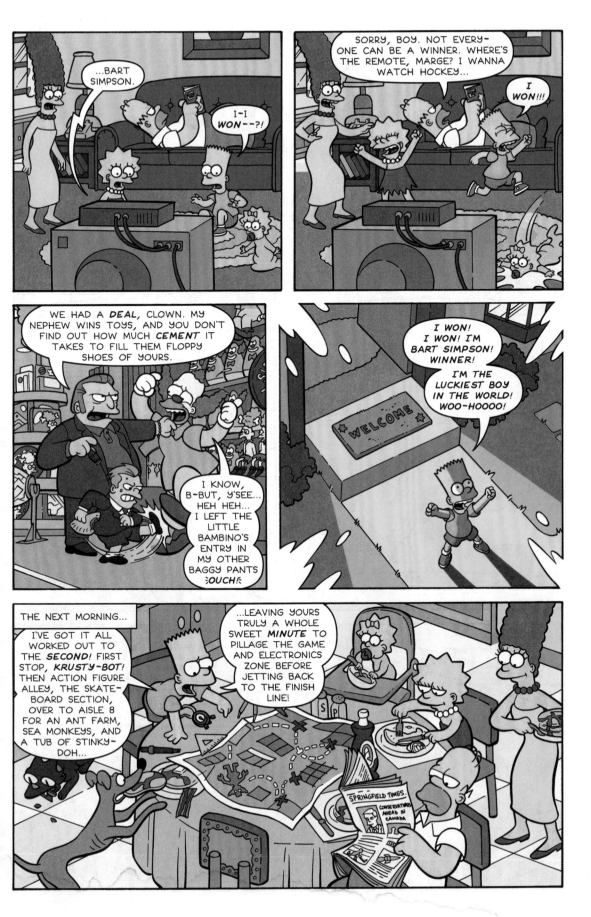

...BART SIMPSON.

I-I WON--?!

SORRY, BOY. NOT EVERY-ONE CAN BE A WINNER. WHERE'S THE REMOTE, MARGE? I WANNA WATCH HOCKEY...

I WON!!!

WE HAD A *DEAL*, CLOWN. MY NEPHEW WINS TOYS, AND YOU DON'T FIND OUT HOW MUCH *CEMENT* IT TAKES TO FILL THEM FLOPPY SHOES OF YOURS.

I KNOW, B-BUT, Y'SEE... HEH HEH... I LEFT THE LITTLE BAMBINO'S ENTRY IN MY OTHER BAGGY PANTS ⁊OUCH⁊

I WON! I WON! I'M BART SIMPSON! WINNER!

I'M THE LUCKIEST BOY IN THE WORLD! WOO-HOOOO!

WELCOME

THE NEXT MORNING...

I'VE GOT IT ALL WORKED OUT TO THE *SECOND!* FIRST STOP, *KRUSTY-BOT!* THEN ACTION FIGURE ALLEY, THE SKATE-BOARD SECTION, OVER TO AISLE 8 FOR AN ANT FARM, SEA MONKEYS, AND A TUB OF STINKY-DOH...

...LEAVING YOURS TRULY A WHOLE SWEET *MINUTE* TO PILLAGE THE GAME AND ELECTRONICS ZONE BEFORE JETTING BACK TO THE FINISH LINE!

SPRINGFIELD TIMES. CONSERVATIVES AHEAD IN CANADA

S P

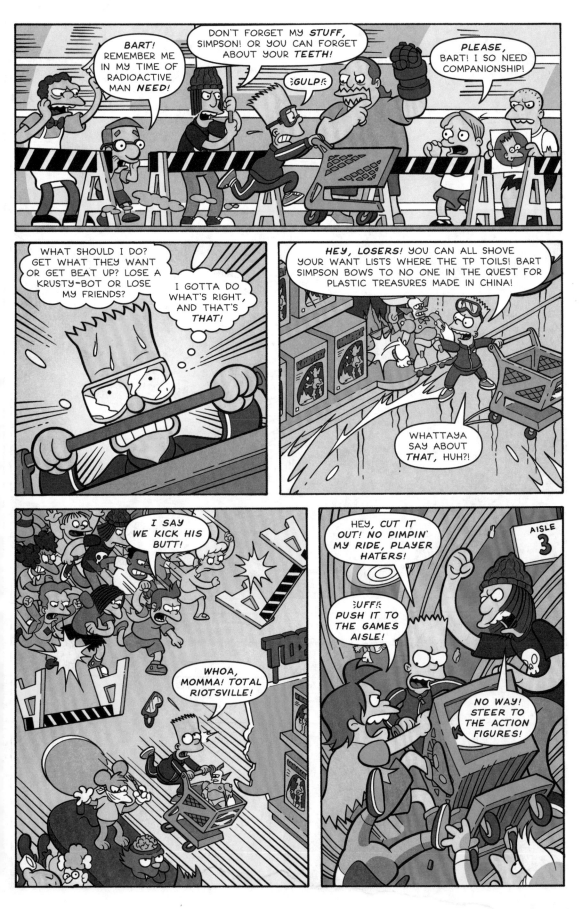

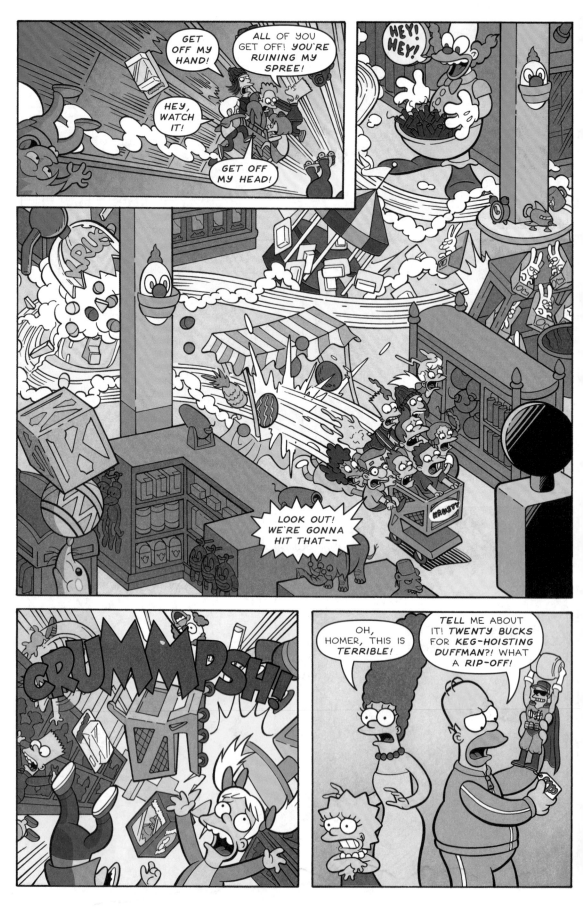

THE TRUE AFICIONADO OF THE POPULAR ARTS WALKS THE WALK, BUT MORE IMPORTANTLY, HE *TALKS THE TALK!* PROPER USAGE OF SCIENCE FICTION, HORROR AND FANTASY QUOTES SEPARATES THE *HE-MEN* FROM THE *LOST BOYS*. IF YOU DON'T KNOW *"THE FORCE IS STRONG IN THIS ONE"* FROM *"THROW ME THE WHIP!"* THEN YOU'RE IN THE LATTER CATEGORY, AND YOU NEED HELP! THEREFORE, I SAY "SUBMITTED FOR YOUR APPROVAL" ARE THESE

HANDY POP CULTURE QUOTES FOR ALL OCCASIONS!

STARTING THE DAY

UP AND ATOM!

RADIOACTIVE MAN, *RADIOACTIVE MAN* #1-PRESENT

SHOPPING

I SEE DEAD PEOPLE.

COLE SEAR, *THE SIXTH SENSE*

AVOIDING DISTRACTIONS

DO YOU HAVE BICLOPS #4?

I'M A TRIFLE DEAF IN THIS EAR, SPEAK A LITTLE LOUDER NEXT TIME.

WILLY WONKA, *WILLY WONKA AND THE CHOCOLATE FACTORY*

APPREHENDING SHOPLIFTERS

YOU'RE UNDER ARREST FOR VIOLATING SECTION 4-1-5-3 OF THE TYCHO TREATY!

AGENT K, *MEN IN BLACK*

EVAN DORKIN
SCRIPT

JEFF BRENNAN
PENCILS

MIKE ROTE
INKS

CHRIS UNGAR
COLORS

KAREN BATES
LETTERS

BILL MORRISON
EDITOR

APPRECIATING THE FINER THINGS

I'D BUY *THAT* FOR A DOLLAR!

"TAKE ME TO YOUR COMIC BOOKS & BASEBALL CARDS"

THE "I'D BUY THAT FOR A DOLLAR" GUY, *ROBOCOP*

LOSING GRACEFULLY

NUCLEAR OPTION

THAT'S IT, MAN! GAME OVER, MAN! GAME OVER!

GAME OVER

PRIVATE W. HUDSON, *ALIENS*

ATTENDING TO NATURE

GAMING CONVENTION   KNIGHT'S ROOM   MAIDEN'S ROOM

I'LL BE BACK.

DUNGEON MASTER

THE T800 TERMINATOR, *TERMINATOR 2*

IDENTIFYING POTENTIAL TROUBLE

BANE BACK   REDJON

EVIL! PURE AND SIMPLE, FROM THE 8TH DIMENSION!

BASE BALL   ITCHY SCRATCHY   BASE BALL   KRUSTY

BUCKAROO BANZAI, *THE ADVENTURES OF BUCKAROO BANZAI ACROSS THE 8TH DIMENSION*

FEELING SUPERIOR

CI-FI-CON

EVEN AMONG MISFITS, YOU'RE MISFITS!

YUKON CORNELIUS, *RUDOLPH THE RED-NOSED REINDEER*

CHOOSING A FILM EXPERIENCE

COMING SOON:
DUDE, WHERE'S MY CAR II
THE SEARCH CONTINUES

BE AFRAID. BE VERY AFRAID.

VERONICA QUAIFE, *THE FLY* (1986 REMAKE)

ADVANCED TIPS

1) VOCALLY IMITATING THE SPEAKER OF THE ORIGINAL QUOTE IS THE SINCEREST FORM OF FANNERY!

2) TAKE THE SUBJECT NOUN IN A QUOTE AND REPLACE IT TO ADAPT TO YOUR NEEDS. FOR EXAMPLE: INSTEAD OF, "IN SPACE NO ONE CAN HEAR YOU SCREAM." (AD CAMPAIGN SLOGAN, *ALIEN*), YOU COULD SAY, "IN *NOISELAND ARCADE*, NO ONE CAN HEAR YOU SCREAM."

WORST TWO PAGE FILLER *EVER*? I THINK *NOT!*

SHOPPING FOR SCHOOL SUPPLIES THE BART SIMPSON WAY!

TONY DIGEROLAMO
SCRIPT

JOHN DELANEY
PENCILS

MIKE ROTE
INKS

CHRIS UNGAR
COLORS

KAREN BATES
LETTERS

BILL MORRISON
EDITOR

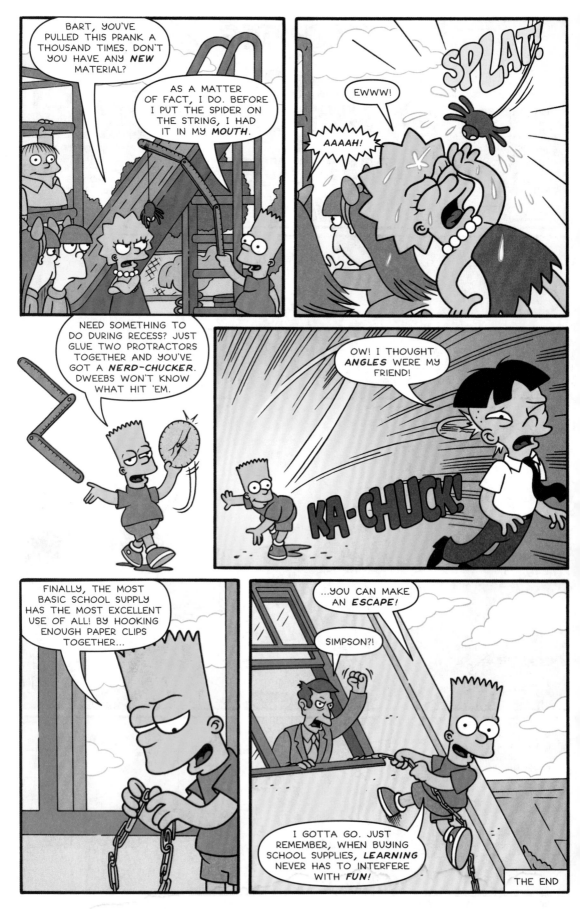

♪GO, GO, GO-GO! MAGGIE AND MOE! ♪

♪ SOLVING A CRIME! DURING PLAYTIME! ♪

THEY'LL PIN THE RAP! THEN IT'S TIME FOR A NAP! ♪ THE COPS NEVER KNOW! IT'S MAGGIE AND MOE! ♪

THE MAGGIE & MOE MYSTERIES!
IN COLOR!

TONIGHT'S EPISODE:
THE DISAPPEARING DUCHESS!

TONY DIGEROLAMO
SCRIPT

JAMES LLOYD
PENCILS

ANDREW PEPOY
INKS

NATHAN HAMILL
COLORS

KAREN BATES
LETTERS

BILL MORRISON
EDITOR

75

PRESENTING EASTERN EUROPE'S FAVORITE CARTOON CAT AND MOUSE TEAM
WORKER AND PARASITE!

JESSE MCCANN
SCRIPT

MIKE ROTE
PENCILS & INKS

NATHAN HAMILL
COLOR

KAREN BATES
LETTERS

BILL MORRISON
EDITOR

THIS IS A STORY ABOUT TWO BEST FRIENDS, A COUNTY FAIR, AND AN ADVENTURE WHERE FUN WAS JUST RIPE FOR THE PICKIN'...

I'M GOING TO TOUCH *EVERYTHING!*

RALPH WIGGUM in HOG TIED

THE MORNING STARTED OUT LIKE AN ORDINARY DAY FOR RALPH AND HIS FAMILY...

ALL RIGHT, *SETTLE DOWN*, RALPHIE. HEH, HEH! DON'T MAKE ME *TASER* YOU.

MAYBE WE SHOULD LET RALPHIE BE A *BIG BOY* TODAY AND LEAVE HIS *LEASH* IN THE CAR.

OKAY, BUT THIS MEANS YOU HAVE TO BE *VERY CAREFUL*, RALPHIE. AND, ALTHOUGH THEY HAVE THE *BEST KINDS OF CANDY*, DON'T TALK TO *STRANGERS*.

AMANDA MCCANN SCRIPT   **JAMES LLOYD** PENCILS   **HOWARD SHUM** INKS   **ART VILLANUEVA** COLORS   **KAREN BATES** LETTERS   **BILL MORRISON** EDITOR

90

MAGGIE SIMPSON in
BABY GOT BACK (AT BURNS)

JESSE McCANN
SCRIPT

JOHN COSTANZA
PENCILS

HOWARD SHUM
INKS

ART VILLANUEVA
COLORS

KAREN BATES
LETTERS

BILL MORRISON
EDITOR

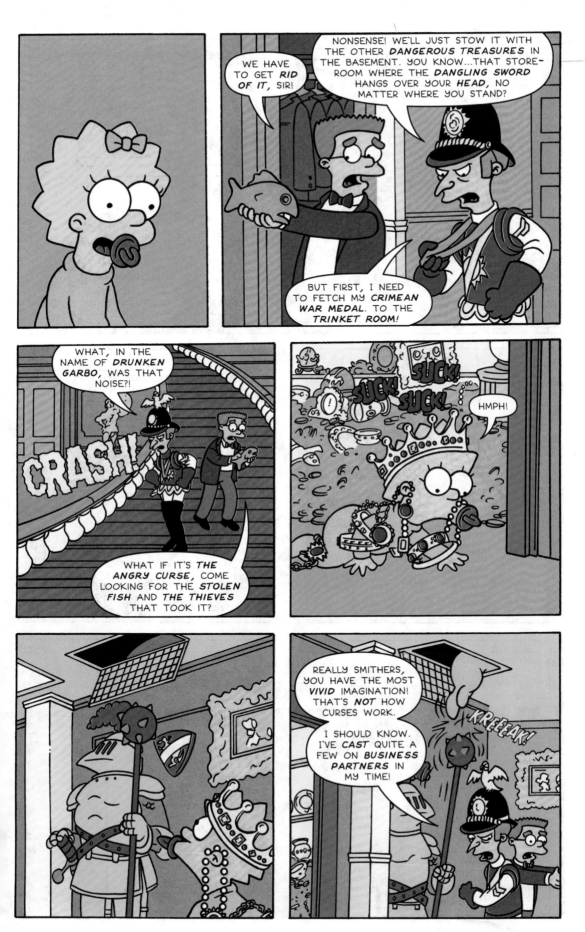

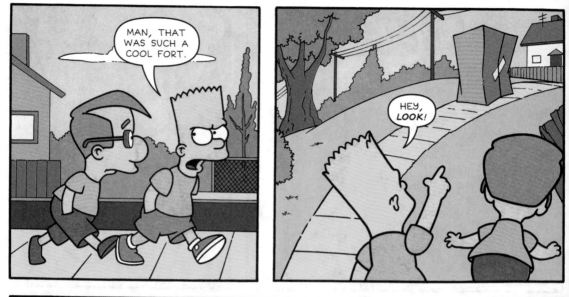

THE END

BART SIMPSON in THE UTER BOMBER

MARY TRAINOR
SCRIPT

JAMES LLOYD
PENCILS

MIKE ROTE
INKS

ART VILLANUEVA
COLORS

KAREN BATES
LETTERS

BILL MORRISON
EDITOR